Hold Fast

PRAISE FOR *HOLD FAST*

The poems that Holly J. Hughes offers us in *Hold Fast* have an elliptical directness, a meditative economy of diction that presents both the bitter and the sweet of our lives, aspects "so intertwined / we can't greet one without the other." Holding fast is the overarching metaphor of this book, like the kelp-binding barnacle with this name, which "lets go what it can, holds fast to all the rest." The poetry of *Hold Fast* brims with pathos-driven energies that celebrate—amidst this life's transitory flux—the "ten thousand sorrows / and ten thousand joys" of human consciousness, human knowledge, and human connectedness, to which we hold fast in the affirmations of these poems.

Carolyne Wright, author of This Dream the World:
New & Selected Poems

Hold Fast, the title of Holly Hughes's latest collection, has a traditional nautical meaning of making a shipboard line "fast," or well-secured, as well as a more general meaning: to "stay true" or "be steady." *Hold Fast*, then, functions as both title and theme. The world, Hughes's poems tell us in clear lines and vivid images, has lost its mooring, been set adrift. While these poems witness the effects of our species' dominance on the earth over the last century, they also reveal compassion. Despite her unflinching portrayal of a degraded planet, many poems in *Hold Fast* are calls for hope, even for celebration and wonder. Hughes asks us as well to "hold fast" through the troubled and rising waters of our times. Often funny, wry, playful—and just as often serious and unsettling—Hughes's poems are deeply moving statements of faith. As a collection, *Hold Fast* is steadfast, entirely true to its title.

Ed Harkness, author of The Law of the Unforeseen

Holly J. Hughes writes poems that live, breathe, and "dance two feelings at once." They shine with gratitude; they are darkened by desire. They struggle against mortality; they bask in its beauty. *Hold Fast* is set in midlife as change ravages family, nation, and the earth, when nostalgia starts pulling the mind one way, yearning the other. And still, Hughes never overlooks the glories of the ordinary, sensory world—an autumn swim in the lake, a tangle of branches brought indoors. I'm so moved by these poems. They've become my companions.

Kathleen Flenniken, author of *Plume*

Holly J. Hughes rekindles a time in America when anything new and exciting and definitely not Midwestern was "enough to feed our longing for life beyond / endless rows of corn." While some of these poems offer refreshing homage to the poets and painters leading her to lament the "daily incremental failings" of this devasting world, other poems heighten the language of science to lyricism while dissecting the "heart-catching joy / and terror" of our lives.

Allen Braden, author of *A Wreath of Down and Drops of Blood*

BOOKS BY HOLLY J. HUGHES

Hold Fast, Empty Bowl Press, 2020.

Passings, Expedition Press, 2016; Wandering Aengus Press, 2019.

Contemplative Approaches to Sustainability in Higher Education: Theory & Practice, Routledge, 2018. Coeditor with Marie Eaton and Jean MacGregor.

Sailing by Ravens, University of Alaska Press, 2014.

The Pen and The Bell: Mindful Writing in a Busy World, Skinner House Press, 2012. With Brenda Miller.

Beyond Forgetting: Poetry and Prose about Alzheimer's Disease, Kent State University Press, 2009. Foreword by Tess Gallagher.

Boxing the Compass, Floating Bridge Press, 2006.

Hold Fast

Holly J. Hughes

EMPTY BOWL

Empty Bowl, founded in 1976 as a cooperative letterpress publisher,
has produced periodicals, broadsides, literary anthologies, collections of
poetry, and books of Chinese translations. As of 2018, our mission is to
publish collections by poets and writers who share Empty Bowl's founding
purpose, "literature and responsibility,"and its fundamental theme, the love
and preservation of human communities in wild places.

Library of Congress Control Number 2019953357

ISBN 9781734187304

EMPTY BOWL
14172 Madrona Drive
Anacortes, Washington 98221

www.emptybowl.org

Printed at Gray Dog Press
Spokane, Washington

Cover and book design: Nina Noble Design

Cover painting: Zann Jacobrown

for my sisters

What will we cling to, in the confusion of the tides?
What structures of connection will hold us in place?

Kathleen Dean Moore, *Holdfast*

CONTENTS

One

Bittersweet,   3

Memory, take me back   4

Hold Fast   6

Square Riggers   8

Pied Piper   9

68th Anniversary of the Bikini   11

Remember the Flood of '65   12

For the Last Roll of Kodachrome   13

The Great Alzana 14

Untethered   15

What Fell   16

Monopoly   17

Will We Make It?   19

Send in the Clown   20

On the 100th Anniversary of the Sinking of the *Titanic*   22

March 6, 1890: Eugene Shieffelin Releases
    80 Starlings in Central Park   24

Nostalgia Redux   26

Two

Late September, Picking Apples   29

Morning Practice   31

Offering of the Fig 33

Consider the Pear   34

Walking Double Bluff   35

North Beach   36

Cape Disappointment   38

Reconsidering Desire   40

Approaching 52   41

Beach School   42

Mind Wanting More   43

E O Y Z P   44

Re-reading Tu Fu Thirty Years Later   46

Shishi Odoshi   47

Holdfast   49

Three

Deconstructing the Peaceable Kingdom   53

Walking the beach with the poets   54

Her Deerness   55

Contemplating Mercy   56

Doors   57

Reading Kooser on the Ferry   58

Walking Gary Snyder's Dog   59

Moon Phases at Deer Park Monastery   61

If the River   62

Mosaic   63

After Seeing *Photograph 51*   64

Adrift   66

Each Bird Singing: A Cento   67

Four

What Daughters Do   71

Subtraction   72

The Bath   74

Whatever Remains   76

Eight Years Later   77

Geometry   78

Measurements   79

Scarlet Hibiscus Blooming   80

Secretariat Redux   81

Walking with Our Fathers   82

Kingfisher's Vigil   83

Meusings   84

Taking Down the Paintings   85

Here, Now, Listen: Letter to Rags from Tieton   87

What You'd Give   89

Five

Credo   93

Pantoum for Tahlequah   94

Against Apocalypse   96

Rising   98

Elemental   99

Heading Home   100

Chimacum Valley Suite   101

One Last Whiff   103

Farm Tour the Day Before Equinox   104

Swimming into Fall   105

After 22 Years, Astilbe   106

Leavings   107

Past Dusk   108

Oak Bay the Last Day of the Year   109

Notes   110

Acknowledgments   112

Gratitude   114

About Holly J. Hughes   115

One

I mistook the gold land for a golden age.

Kathleen Flenniken,
"Letter to Rilke"

*Now more than ever you can be
generous toward each day
that comes, young, to disappear
forever, and yet remain
unaging in the mind.*

Wendell Berry,
"No Going Back"

Bittersweet,

my mother called it, filling the back
of the station wagon with tangled branches,

the only way she knew to bring what's wild
inside the tidy rooms of her colonial.

How could I know it would trail me
all these years with its bright eyes?

Sweetbitter, Sappho called it,
knew too well the heart's grammar—

that the tang of cherries lingers
longer than the sweet,

that the ripe fig sweetens as
its skin begins to pucker.

It is just they are so intertwined
we can't greet one without the other:

one's bright twin, one's lengthening shadow.

Memory, take me back

to the cricket *chirr* of Minnesota afternoons
to that white farmhouse with peeling paint,
splintered wood picnic table, crockery brimming
with potato salad, deviled eggs, marionberry pies,

murrey juices bubbling as they're carried out
from the dim kitchen, counter crowded
with pans of homemade rolls, flour dusting
the wood butcher block, drifting down

onto worn linoleum. Take me back to days that stretched
like rows of corn, to that girl in braids who had
to be told to stop racing up the rows—
yes, you there—to come to the table to eat

with the grown-ups who looked more grown-up
than she could imagine, women in faded
cotton dresses, sturdy black shoes, seamed stockings,
no matter 100-degree heat. And while we're there

tell me, what was that girl thinking as she excused
herself, swung a skinny tanned leg over the bench
to dash once more down the harrowing rows,
sure she could hear the sheathed ears whisper

to her, then retreat to the beanpole house
where the beans offered their pendulous green bodies
to be picked & snapped into heavy blue bowls.
Make room not just for swinging from a long

knotted rope to drop, breathless, into cold water
at the gravel pit, but for these memories, too,
still glowing like silent ghosts, for those stoic
farm women we never listened to enough,

inscrutable *shushing* of the corn and beans.

Hold Fast

i.
All those seasons climbing
what others rigged, never
trusting what was hers,

what she could hold to
once aloft. What she knew:
slap of sail before wind,

winch tight, released,
line playing out endlessly
through empty hands.

Make it fast, skipper shouts.
And she did. Still does. Still
leaps when others cry out.

ii.
When did the body become a vessel others ride in?

iii.
What happened that night—
memory or dream—and she
too young, *will never know.*

Stairs creaking, he climbed
into the musty attic, carried
the sooty lantern, paused

at the threshold, whispered
her name—*to check on her
she still wants to believe*—stood

too long, then blew it out.

Square Riggers

Here in Todos Santos, hot sun dries sheets in an hour,
maybe less. I hoist the basket of sopping clothes, drops

exploding in thirsty dust, reach into the child's red cotton dress
on the hanger for wooden clothespins—not the kind that spring open,

but the old ones that need to be clamped down hard—
clothespins we painted with faces for puppet shows

behind sheets billowing in the wind off the prairie, where
we watched my grandmother hang out the wash, giggled

as she hung my grandfather's cotton briefs. *Did I decide then not to grow up?*
I never tried on my mother's lipstick, never wanted to slip across

that border, played Kick the Can until long past dusk; but now,
without thinking, I slip the clothespins between my lips, hands free

to hang each sheet to the line, look down the cotton clothesline,
see not my mother's firm biceps, but my grandmother's sagging flesh,

then lift and slide the next wooden pin from my lips, clamp it down
hard in honor of her, lips pursed, all she could never say. Meanwhile, I

threw my lot in with sailors, square riggers sailing before the wind,
forgetting these sheets billowing across the prairie until today,

drawing me round the buoy toward a life I get to choose.

Pied Piper

Once a week, the band played at the band shell,
and we hopped on our Schwinns after dinner, rode

ten minutes down the lakefront to save seats.
When the man with the mask appeared, we kicked

off our sneakers to follow him, machine on his back,
lurching down the aisles, smoke billowing

like a magic act so we could listen to the shrill
cry of piccolo, not the curse & swat of mosquitoes.

Our parents never knew—*or did they?* —that
we followed the machine with its billowing

haze because our older brothers and sisters
followed. We followed because the smoke

smelled sweet, forbidden. We followed
because that's what we knew: to follow

the Pied Piper of convenience, one more way
to make the world safe for humans, one more win

for science over biting nature. We followed not knowing
we were following the Pied Piper of cancer,

of genetic mutation, of egg shells too thin to hatch,
of frogs born without testicles. We breathed it all in—

that seductive haze of progress—and today,
DDT winds quietly, deep in our DNA.

68th Anniversary of the Bikini

July 17, 2014

Growing up in the 60s, I knew the bikini
as what my friends and I wore strapped
to our flat chests—nothing yet to hide,

nothing between us and our Coppertone tans.
Oh, we slathered on the baby oil, glistening
like slick linoleum in the hot Midwest sun.

We didn't know it as a revolutionary act, wearing
this skimpy suit, *so small it could pass through
a wedding ring*—the ad when it first came out—

invented by Louis Reard to stir things up after the war,
we just knew the song that played on the radio:
she wore an itsy bitsy teenyweeny yellow polka dot bikini

and sang along, vamping it up. We didn't know
that it was named after the atoll where the first
bomb was tested, though I remember wondering—

ah, the innocence of youth—why the atoll was named
after a swimsuit. We didn't know that fallout
from atomic testing slowly poisoned those

on nearby islands, that strontium would
honeycomb our bones as we've long since
outgrown our bikinis, now worry about osteoporosis,

in fact, can hardly recall wearing a bikini at all.

Remember the Flood of '65

when we made bologna sandwiches for the men
working on the levee pouring cold sand
into burlap bags, men who worked against rising
waters of the Mississippi, doctors and lawyers
elbow to elbow with truck drivers and plumbers,
all men with kids at home. *The men will save us*

our mothers promised, as they turned
to what they could do: make food.
I was 10, *old enough to help*, my mother said,
so I slathered French's mustard on limp
slices of Wonder Bread, passed them
down for bologna, where they were slipped

into wax paper sleeves and sent off with heavy
thermoses of Folgers so thin it looked like tea.
That year we moved the davenport upstairs,
took up the carpets. What if the levee broke?
No one spoke of it, but I knew the river
could take our house, wanted to reclaim

its ancient riverbed before it was trapped—
for our convenience—into a lake, back
when engineers could fix every mistake
with a sharp #2 pencil and slide rule.
Yes, the engineers saved us then,
the levee held. But the river remembers,
will someday spread wide her muddy
arms, reclaim her rightful bed.

For the Last Roll of Kodachrome

December 29, 2010

It's official: *No more Kodachrome Moments.*
No more kids wearing Mickey Mouse ears
at Disneyland, no more families at Mt. Rushmore
mugging for Dad's camera. So long to all that.

So long to crew cuts and plaid Bermuda shorts.
So long to madras and muumuus. So long
to anklets, knee socks, bell bottoms,
peasant shirts and Birkenstocks.

So long to the company that employed thousands
but poisoned the waters with the chemical
brew needed to permanently fix
each happy moment to glossy paper.

So long to sitting down to Christmas dinner,
table laid with polished silver and Italian goblets,
lit candles guttering amid fir boughs, while
we smile patiently at my father holding

the flash high like a reporter, wait
for the blue bulb to blind us, but it doesn't
flash and our eyes roll as he, rueful,
advances the film. So long to that, too.

So long to companies we trust, to the people
who believed those ads, who kept grinning
for the camera, still believing happiness
possible in each long, obedient moment.

The Great Alzana

Sometimes you feel you haven't given people enough.
I feel I have to fall and break my neck for them.

obituary of Howard Davis in the *New York Times,* Sept. 2002

As though the wire weren't thin enough, 5/8″ cable forty feet in the air.
He wanted no safety net, skipping down mortality's shimmering line,

breaking bones so many times —-*arms, legs, ribs, ankles and his back*—
that New York law required a net for aerial acts more than 25 feet.

At 14, he saws down a neighbor's tree, sticks it in the ground,
runs a cable to his own tree, learns to walk the high wire

under the waxing moon, earns 100 pounds at a fair in Sheffield,
goes to work for Ringling, then Barnum. He learns to jump

rope forward, back, blindfolded, is the first to carry three people
on a bicycle. *What else can he do?* He runs the wire each night,

trembling under the hot lights, darkness thick and yawning,
no net below. *What else can he give them?*

He retires in his 70s but keeps his high wire—still no net—
in the backyard until his heart won't brook it. Even then,

when the moon was full, his wife said, *he'd climb the ladder*
and just sit there. Some nights she says she sees him still,

running his wire under the waning moon,
nothing left to give, nothing left to break or lose.

Untethered

That morning, the headline about the astronaut
who drove nine hundred miles wearing a diaper
to confront her love interest's love interest.

The astronaut met her plane, tailed her to the car,
rapped on the window. When she began to cry,
the love interest rolled it down, called the police.

In the astronaut's car, they find the evidence:
a Buck knife, rubber tubing, Hefty garbage bags,
the box of diapers. The story didn't say

they all wore diapers in space. That maybe
she imagined this voyage like all the others:
leaving the atmosphere, weightlessness

of love, days without gravity to tether her to earth.
And though we wonder how is it that someone
so rational — *an astronaut!* —would lose it

so completely, if we squirm as we read this,
perhaps we suspect there's an astronaut
inside each of us that dreams of blasting off,

of being that untethered, that lost in space.

What Fell

After the planes struck the steel girders
designed to withstand 1,000 degrees,
after the passengers called home
on their cell phones, after the oxygen
masks released on impact, after the brokers
sent a last email, after they ran for the stairs
with secretaries and custodians, after they turned
back for the blue promise of windows, after they jumped
into nothingness, hands clasped, after the coffee pots,
the African violets, the photos of children were inhaled
by the ravenous mouth of flame, after the firefighters
climbed the stairs, axes flat against their chests
like crucifixes, after the waterfall of flames and steel,
after the locked file cabinets released their contents
—resumes, bills, invoices—shreds drifted down like snow,
three inches deep on the graves at St. Paul's,
fell on the school yards and for days the children,
not knowing how much they would need to believe
in civilization, picked them all up.

Monopoly

The boot booted
wheelbarrow wheeled
out, thimble thumbed

down. *To be replaced by a T-rex,*
a penguin, and a rubber ducky, says
Parker Brothers, will not travel down

tradition's track. One extinct
species followed by the soon-to-be
extinct; two obsolete replaced

by one ubiquitous. But voted
in—and out—by The People.
What about that out-of-era top

hat? Didn't it clutch its cane,
exit stage left decades back?
Didn't we ditch decorum then?

And when will we nix,
deep-six the battleship?
What to make of this trading in

of tradition for what's trending
this day, this hour, this millennium?
How to pass along our brave old world?

We leave the Scottie with the cat circling
the board, buying up Park Place, Boardwalk,
all the railroads, while we, distracted

by our 24-hour news feeds, can't make a move.

Will We Make It?

Mary Tyler Moore left this week, quietly closing
the door on the set as she did decades ago,
with a tearful smile. No tossing her tam in the air,
no spunky rejoinders to Murray. I want to believe

she smiled that endearing smile one more time,
but no one can tell us, the 12-inch B&W
set with its handy on/off button
packed off with the fondu pot.

Mike Connors strode off the set last week,
tough private eye who knew Right from Wrong,
called Truth as he saw it, crooked smile seducing
us, back when masculine men still could.

Then Barbara Hale snapped shut her clutch,
that able secretary on *Perry Mason*—we all knew
she ran the place. I want to believe
they're together now, dusting off the TV set,

fluffy slippers on, bowl of butter-sopped
popcorn passing hand to greasy hand,
watching reruns, remembering what seems
like better days but were really just for some.

Send in the Clown

Barnum & Bailey to close its tent after more than 100 years

January 2017

We were innocent, easily seduced by the exotic,
so when the circus rolled into our Midwest town
in August's heat, we lined up for seats.

High wire act lower, trapeze artists
in tandem, not troupes, calliope music careened
off-key, no hi-tech lights glaring at halftime

but enough to stir our longing for life beyond
straight rows of corn. Not just one act
but three: the couple who grasped glistening

wrists midair, girl in spangled tights who spun
arabesques, horse cantering like a toy around the ring,
lion padding up to roar like MGM.

Too easy, then, to overlook the anger
in the lion's roar, desperation in the tiger's pacing,
indignation in the elephant's stomp.

They're gone now. We went back
to worrying about crops. Maybe the mill lost
a few workers, maybe a car mechanic traded

in his socket set, but life returned
to what we took as normal,
setting blinders on our horses again.

Tonight the girl's tattoos look ordinary, high wire
acts what we watch on YouTube. See now only
animals cowering under the cruel whip.

Let them go. Release the lions from their roaring,
tigers from their pacing, horses from their circling.
Release the couple from their soaring bar, ringmaster

from his manic speech, clown from his baggy pants,
girl from her submissive steed. Let them go
home; they've served their purpose.

But let Feste stand alone at the center,
real tears streaking his greasy cheeks
at the three-ring circus we've become.

On the 100th Anniversary of the Sinking of the *Titanic*

for Wallace Hartley, bandmaster

We've seen the movies, sung the song,
tried to imagine—beyond Hollywood's rendition—
the *ship that would never go down.*

But it did: stern sank first, bow thrust up
like a skyscraper, lights winking in each stateroom
until the generators sizzled, slid into

the sea. Meanwhile, the slow, confused rush
for lifeboats, women & children, first class first,
those in steerage left below to pray.

Most accounts blame the captain: he was indecisive,
muster weak, lifeboats launched half-empty;
radioman ignored warnings, radioed the wrong position.

They say he went down with the ship, listening
to the wind-snatched notes of "Nearer My God to Thee"
though even that story may be fantasy.

In the end, it was the musicians who cared
for the passengers, turning to their art
to sustain them, though it didn't keep

them afloat in the frigid waves
of the North Atlantic, didn't bring them
home to their families, ticker tape parades.

One hundred years later, we try to imagine
not those lucky in the lifeboats,
but those who stayed on deck

stroking a violin, prelude to
the cold sea snapping shut
like a purse, playing music

that won't save anyone,
each note hanging
in the insubstantial air.

March 6, 1890: Eugene Shieffelin Releases 80 Starlings in Central Park

I'll have a starling shall be taught / To speak nothing but "Mortimer"
and give it him / To keep his anger still in motion.

Shakespeare, *Henry IV,* Part 1

Snow has shaken loose all morning,
nesting in the crotch of the ailanthus,
streaking the black trunks of the locust.

Upstate, currant farmers worry
about the freeze. In the city,
fathers hitch horses to sleighs.

He hugs his wool coat tighter,
spirals his muffler,
lurching along, cobblestones

slick under four inches of snow,
in each hand a cage, balanced
to a scale of justice.

Behind him a kite tail of servants carry
eighty starlings—imported from Europe
to improve the landscape—stutter in protest.

At last, he stops, lowers the cages, lifts each latch.
The starlings step out blinking,
claw feet unscrolling in snow.

Dazed from months aboard ship
and carriage, they linger near the cages,
flex their wings, a spattering of white on black,

like puddingstone, lower their tails,
cock their heads, preen,
eyes bright like honey.

At 4:30 clouds cut away,
clear sky thickens into evening.
Still they stay next to their cages.

Finally, growing cold, he rushes at the birds,
scarecrowing his arms: *Go, go, go.*
At first one, then another, and another,

until the whole murmuration lifts
and spirals, a spidery helix
against a darkening sky.

Nostalgia Redux

March out the cliches, Hallmark greetings, soft focus lens. Line up
the grandparents, ask about telegraphs, telegrams, dial telephones.
Where have all the phone booths gone, receivers dangling, phone books
fled, no dial tone.

Who will believe us? *That's how it was, once.* Yes, we admit:
collectively, we rolled our eyes, looked the other way,
knew it wasn't right, sighed, did it anyway. *Too much
to do, can't be bothered, not enough, too much at stake.*

History comes into focus when we finally rein in, look
back, see what we can't when we're in it. When
do the old ways become just old, not stories told,
sparks searing an empty night, to hold at bay the dark?

When will nostalgia, that hopeless Siren, stop winking in the rearview?
Yes, a golden age for the rich, the born right, the lucky, the white.
Rust shimmers as it oxidizes, burnished by time; until then,
maybe it's just the corrosive truth of rust.

Two

Then the world is that actress from a Sanskrit poem,
whose greatness was showing two feelings at once.

Jane Hirshfield, *The Lives of the Heart*

Late September, Picking Apples

for Dave

Maples drift toward fall across the valley,
red veins creep, green leaves seep to yellow.
Below, Lake Chelan draped in gauze;
on the hillside, apples wait on sturdy limbs.

Back from a lean season, we pick apples
to pay for our stay. I drag the wood ladder
to a gnarled trunk, set three legs in soft earth,
apex vanishing into the constellation of Galas.

I square my shoulders, canvas bag loose like an
apron across my chest, cinch the drawstring tight,
climb each flat rung high into the crispness
of fall. Learn to reach for one apple at a time,

twist its umbilical until it releases, ease
each apple into the canvas sack, reach
measuring the span of my domain, fall's
fleeting circumference. Wobble down

the ladder pregnant with apples, empty
the sack with a tug of knotted rope, listen
for the quiet thuds. Back on the ladder,
a new radius: reach, drop, palm round

firmness of apple by heart until I can reach
and drop like breath, inhaling apples, chill, fall,
exhaling sun, salmon, summer, muscles tightening
to hold the bag open, willing the heart to open

to whatever fall will bring. Meanwhile,
summer's last promise glistens
like the lake below, all that eludes,
the one apple forever just out of reach.

Morning Practice

i.
This morning, sky lightening to the east
where the Cascades rest in their robes of snow.

Tell me, how is it these mountains can stand still,
so quiet, so long? Next door, a cat glides down

the back stairs, stalking a crow. A woman waits,
draped in a rain hood, tapping a white cane.

Last night, the dancer in the wheelchair never
moved her legs once but spun and spun

in a bright helix of light. Then the last piece
when the dancer said he wanted to dance

two feelings at once—the movement and the rest
within the movement—and he did, his body

holding both tenderly, as if it were easy
as if it could be possible.

ii.
Sometimes I can't sleep for the straight-grained fir
that frames this cabin, veins like ribbon candy running

down the windowsills, a few knots, not many,
and stunning where they occur: a sinkhole, grain swirling

like sand around a drift log, scar of limbs lost, growth
not to be messed with. I know what it's like to

split straight-grained fir, *like butter*, loggers say,
axe sinking deep and true on its first overhead arc,

resonant crack as the fibers spring apart, loosing
their grip, sighing a bit. And I know what it's like to

strike the knots, ring of axe blade against fists
dense as stone, then letting the blade find its way

around each knot, knowing that's where
the tongues of the fire will hold, enthralled.

Offering of the Fig

Always the fig splays open its leaves,
gathers the sun in lobed mitts
while the flower turns inward,
scent of frankincense and myrrh.

Small seeds seek the quiet source
as the nomads rode months in the desert
to arrive at the green island where water
was offered up by the earth,

as the camel carries water,
as the urn carries absence,
as the ship, abandoned,
carries only its ribs and air,

as the heart rides from what
it cannot yet bear to carry.

This, too, the fig promises,
its mule-ear skin breaking,
releasing dark flower into day,
wet and trembling in your hands.

Consider the Pear

What if Eve had offered a pear instead of an apple?
A pear with its tender, bruised skin, swelling,
voluptuous bottom, juice that dribbles your chin,
a pear ripe for maybe ten minutes
before going gritty on your tongue.

A *Bosc,* perhaps, or *D'Anjou* that Adam would eat slowly,
not the crisp eagerness of apple, its chaste white flesh,
thin red wrap of skin, five perfect seeds orbiting
the core like moons which we don't eat,
remembering our mother's warnings.

But the pear can all be eaten, from the bottom
all the way up the thick, curved stem.
Would this earth wobble more elliptically
in its orbit if ripeness were our way?
Not the concentric spin of night

to day in perfect hemispheres, not the easy
crunch of fall, predictable, like oak leaves
underfoot, but a shape that stalls
its spinning, so summer lingers,
grows fuller each day, hangs

on its abundant stem,
blushes mottled rose,
swells at night
under the full moon,
turning round and round,

wanting only
to be picked
by you.

Walking Double Bluff

Again, above the cliff, the red biplane soars,
arcs, rolls, turns over under the endless sky—

not exactly like a hawk, its single-hearted plummet,
or osprey's steady soar, or two crows, splayed black

wing to wing tip, or two eagles, talons clenched, spinning out,
or even geese, their chatty, undulating route—

but close as we'll come, light glinting on wings
like code for those of us below, restless to know

that language in our bodies like the blind know Braille,
the dips and turns of its feathered ways, its unfettered words.

North Beach

Together we watch two girls ride their horses
into the Straits, legs clamped like wishbones

to the rolling, muscled sea of each horse's back:
a chestnut, a dappled roan. On land, watch

as they turn each animal's head back
toward the sea, reins taut against the neck,

eyes white, nostrils flaring, relinquishing
will in froth of sea foam.　　　I want to hold

that moment, imperceptible, when hooves
leave the cobbled beach, when the horses lean

forward, legs churning, necks surging ahead,
circling back to land, hooves staccato

on stone as they scramble ashore, then
circle back to the sea, water streaming

off their bodies, each splash filling
with sun. With each circling, the girls

return to what they know: press of thigh
against muscled back, salt on lips,

tangle of wind and sun, not yet
separate from their bodies,

the dazzling, devastating world
they soon enough will enter.

Cape Disappointment

Maybe a day like this when Lewis and Clark reached the Pacific,
no more basalt cliffs to scale, swollen rivers to ford,

just shore pines hunched in wind, rain-sopped moss and beyond,
long curls of sea unscrolling, shattering white on rock. The Pacific

at last, but not the end of the journey. I imagine them peeling off
sweaty buckskin, dashing into the surf, Seaman between them,

the Corps lined up, maybe mustering a jig. But it was November,
the storm raged all week. They hunkered down at Dismal Nitch,

sea's incessant grumble beneath, tent restive in wind, riven with rain,
debated where to winter. They couldn't know the worst lay ahead, then

the long trek back across the continent. Here's what I want to know:
for how long was the Pacific the shimmering ring they could at last

reach out and grab, before they turned their backs on her shining face,
settled into the dripping moss, dried their soaked boots

by the fire, ocean now a mumbling counterpoint?
The destination glittering out there but still, kindling to gather,

a reluctant fire to fan, that irritating sliver in the thumb?
A disappointment, Clark wrote in his journal. Was it

just all those miles to reel back to their lives? I rise early,
pack the car, no time for another walk along the sea.

Disappointment trails like an orphan, fetching up
with long-stuffed grievances: that ill-fitting coat, turned

bottle of wine, even the man you love who lets you down
in ways too petty to name. All the way home, in the rear

view, that seductive sea, her gold ring shimmering.

Reconsidering Desire

Today the trees barely move, sky a study in grey.
But above the horizon, a blue opening that just now

closes. *Give up desire*, said the Buddha. Surely, that's
not what he meant. Yes, a dewdrop world.

But the bowl of lemons, tart cherries, pomegranate, too?
And what about that ruby glint in winter's drowsy sleep?

Even happy as you think you surely must be,
you can't help imagine that path vanishing

into dark firs where sunlight glints, then
shatters, bright shards at your feet.

Approaching 52

She realizes she'll never be a lion-tamer, tall hat and curling whip,
lions and tigers padding in circles on huge, silent paws,

she's too late for Jacques Cousteau, balanced on the edge
of the boat, strapped into steel lungs, tilting back into the sea,

she won't become a wildlife photographer, packing
cameras in the Himalayas in search of the snow leopard,

that even though her mother said *you can be anything you want, dear*
at some point the trajectory soaring up begins to arc

down. Still, she dreams: Barnum & Bailey pull into town
at midnight, *rasp and skreetch* as cage doors yawn to release

the big cats, earth shakes as the elephants, freed,
stomp, trunk to tail, down Main Street.

Beach School

Blue lounge chairs lined up like desks face the sea.
We know the sea speaks in tongues, but still we cup

an ear, hope to snag a word, even one letter
we could clamber aboard, maybe an A or H,

anything to keep from drifting off like the osprey
vanishing into an empty sky. We want it to add

up to something resembling wisdom or even just
something we can believe in. Royal terns tack

in the wind, orange beaks aligned, a scoop
of pelicans descends, all bills and wings. When did

the waves begin to ebb, when did possibility
quit waving like an old friend, start going

down, no life ring around? Listen for each
wave's whisper: this life not what you'd imagined,

your safe life, its muttering undertow of grief.

Mind Wanting More

Only a beige slat of sun
above the horizon, like a shade
pulled not quite down. Otherwise,
clouds. Sea rippled here and
there. Birds reluctant to fly.
The mind wants a shaft of sun to
stir the grey porridge of clouds,
an osprey to stitch sea to sky
with its barred wings, some dramatic
music: a symphony, perhaps
a Chinese gong.

But the mind always
wants more than it has—
one more bright day of sun,
one more clear night in bed
with the moon; one more hour
to get the words right; one
more chance for the heart in hiding
to emerge from its thicket
in dried grasses—as if this quiet day
with its tentative light weren't enough,
as if joy weren't strewn all around.

EOYZP

The letters march across the wall.
Can you read the next line? I squint
to bring the ragtag troop into focus,
not wanting to fail even this exam.

He zooms his blinding light into each eye
once, again, sits down, leans back.
Cataracts, he says, no expression
on his young, impassive face.

I think *cold water, a mountainside,*
spray on my face, my brain not
connecting with this word I've
hitched up to the cart of old people.

Did you spend a lot of time outside?
All those years at sea, watching sun
waltz with water, not knowing
beauty would exact a price.

He tips my head back, squeezes a drop
into each eye to check for glaucoma,
releases me into a November night.
Every streetlight, then, a starburst

as I make my way to the dock,
watch the ferry loom larger,
its blurred city of lights, imagine
a future forever out of focus,

think then of Van Gogh's stars,
Monet's lily pads, how they both
knew this world more luminous
than these daily, incremental failings.

Re-reading Tu Fu Thirty Years Later

Somewhere it's still spring in the mountains.
All these years I've come alone, seeking you,

far off in your land, your own century. You took
to the road with your quill pen, emptied

a bottle each night with friends, still rose
at dawn to write your bittersweet poems

that ring, temple bells across these centuries.
For years I imagined I might find you

wandering the jagged ridge, catch you
and Li Po late some night, drunk

on the cold moon. Tell me, who
was the *you* in that poem I committed

to memory at twenty-two, seeking
a life other than my own?

So many seasons to see what's here.
And so many years later, who is the *you*

that still wants to become you, even
knowing now what it means:

an empty boat, drifting?

Shishi Odoshi

for Sue

Listen: how smoothly
stream slips over stones
downhill to where
hollow bamboo waits

for cool water
to fill its dry throat
then the *thok*
against stone

as it dips like
a heron darting
for fish, fast,
a simple movement

to frighten the boars
that roamed the gardens
of the Zen monks
in the 14th century.

Six centuries later I listen
to the sound of emptiness
filling until it pivots, the
molecule of water

that carries it over
no different from the rest
but the movement quick
as the heart without mind.

Empty and fill,
fill and empty,
neither first nor last
but flowing together,

the movement of filling
carrying the emptying,
as the hollow vase
carries air

as the heart empties
and fills each day with
ten thousand sorrows
and ten thousand joys.

Holdfast

Last week of August: too soon for falling
leaves, fog that rises at dawn, ghosts up
the beach, geese lining up in their ragtag V.

Beyond the sandstone ledge carved
like a torso by the waves, beyond
purple sea stars inching toward tide pools,

ribbons of bull kelp drift with the tide,
ebb and flow, anchored to the sea floor
by a half-inch barnacle called a *holdfast*.

It knows the principle of hunkering down,
riding out the storm, staying put. All
winter, beneath the sea's relentless chop

it holds fast, gives over to each storm,
flows with each rising tide. All winter
it lets go what it can, holds fast to the rest.

That's what we'll do come November.
Hold fast to what sustains: our friends,
a steaming bowl of soup, this beach.

Three

When the bird and the book disagree,
always believe the bird.

James J. Audubon

Maybe we're here only to say: house,
bridge, well, gate, jug, olive tree, window...
but to say them, remember,
oh, to say them in a way that the things themselves
never dreamed of existing so intensely.

Rilke, *The Duino Elegies*

Deconstructing the Peaceable Kingdom

It first comes up in Bible School—
the wild-maned lion lies down with the lamb—

and I flip to that dog-eared page, want it to be so.
All through grade school, I know it still could happen,

rescue spiders, believe cat and mouse a game,
even as my cat slinks into the field.

Then Jack London insists *red in tooth and claw*,
but I'm rooting for Buck, not the man.

I learn to read literature as symbol, what blood
represents, understand the *Natural Order of Things*.

Personification means giving human qualities to animals,
my teacher says, *which of course they can't have*.

I want to describe the deer with her liquid eyes
as *lonely* until I learn that's *really* pathetic.

That's when Modern shows up, all edges and angles.
Irony taps its cool foot in the wings. Postmodern

follows, Signifier close on his heels, language loosed
from its leash, words drifting into a sky

I still could swear is blue.

Walking the beach with the poets

each morning at dawn, sandpipers skittering
        before the waves, when along they come,
           ready with their advice:

Careful, Elizabeth warns, *don't frighten them.*
        But look at the way they run, finical, awkward. Whatever
           are they looking for? Something, something…

How graceful the small before danger! Ted notes,
        pacing the beach, his shirt tail lifting like a balloon
           until he's aloft, off on another poem.

Tom follows, wading into the surf, *I grow old, I grow old,*
        I shall wear the bottoms of my trousers rolled,
           muttering about peaches.

Elizabeth returns, notes the color of each grain of sand
        (no detail too small), invokes poets long ago,
           sees metaphors all around.

I stand beside her, strain to hear the waves *hiss like fat,*
        see this sandpiper as a student of Blake.
           But all I hear are waves.

All I see is this sandpiper,
        more substantial than any of us,
           knowing in each hollow bone he belongs.

Her Deerness

This deer that just showed up at the
Writing in the Wild workshop at Doe Bay
has not arrived for us, though we want

to think she has, bounding up on pogo stick legs
as we discuss the last line of Galway Kinnell's
"St. Francis and the Sow": *Does leaving the article*

off give the word sow more "sowness?" This deer
is not here to teach us anything—that
would be anthropocentric—as we all learned

in graduate school. This deer drops
to her bony knees in the green grass, lowers
her body, belly plump with windfall apples,

legs folding like a card table; this deer
settles down to listen as we talk of paying
attention to nature, look at papers

with words, not at this deer who is offering
her body for our study, *deerness* shining
from every cell of her hard hooves,

quivering black nose, twitching tail,
her language we keep saying
we want to understand.

Contemplating Mercy

From a distance, we watch the gull hop,
dragging one wing like a shipwrecked sail

toward the safety of beach grass,
desperate because he knows my dog wants

to jerk free of his leash, run up the beach,
find the gull—*now tipped back,*

beak opening without sound—
wants to sniff him over, take

those long feathers in his mouth,
both wings now broken free, working

like twin sails to lift off. Above,
two gulls circle and call. I pull

on the leash, lead my dog toward
sandpipers running before

the cold advance of waves—
a ruse that works for now.

And the gull, spent, flops
onto its back, contemplates

mercy, blue vagaries of sky.

Doors

for Robert Hedin

Solid doors of cherry
hang in every doorway,
eight feet tall, they lean
into the room when called,
swing close with a polite
whisper, block out the
the bathroom light
land snug against
the jamb with a
silent bow, enough
of a statement—
no need to say more—
not full of hollow
promises, laminated
with fancy veneers
that peel and split
but the real thing
that knows when to close
and when to open.

Reading Kooser on the Ferry

Hot for us. Hot enough to sit outside on deck
in shirtsleeves. Children race up and down
metal-grated stairs, trying to catch seagulls
gliding as if on strings above the rails.

A couple circumnavigates the ferry,
he gripping a knobby, varnished cane, she frail
in a flowered cotton housedress and cardigan.
Everyone else in T-shirts, flipflops, aerodynamic
shades. I leaf through your book, looking for
a blank page they might have sprung from,
watch, waiting for the long glide across
the floor, the shy, courtly bow.

Walking Gary Snyder's Dog

for Gary Snyder

I didn't expect a poodle for this poet—a working dog,
perhaps a border collie, a shepherd, or even a husky—

but she's a poodle, standard, compact, wiry, and smart,
like him, and right now she's ready to run. She pulls

me up the street, past the arcade with fake putting greens,
past the colliding bumper cars, the Slurpees and Sno-Cones,

past the kids licking soft serve. She's tracking a scent,
races from bush to bush: sniff & pee, sniff & pee, lifts

her handsome head to test the wind, trots up the street,
sure-footed, sure that following these whiffs will add up

to a life well spent. Just when I think I have her under
control, she trees a squirrel, strains to chase the deer browsing

in a rose bed, but the deer just looks at her, drops its head,
resumes chewing, rose petals spilling from its mouth.

She cocks her head, reconsiders. We cut through
an alley, cross a yard to reach the stream

where she wades up to her belly in cold water,
drinks deep. On the way back to his Subaru,

she pauses at each prospect, then chooses

the best manicured green lawn to squat and poop.

Here's my dilemma: Do I leave it, Gary Snyder's dog's poop?
Will they view it as he might: the best fertilizer around?

Nature or Culture? Ghost wildness wafting its pungent scent
even here in this tourist town? I want to say I leave it

steaming on the green grass, last token of our lost animal
nature, sure he'd approve this act of civic disobedience.

I find a piece of plastic blowing up the street,
stoop to scoop, return her to the car.

Learn the smells, she pants in parting. *Go light.*

Moon Phases at Deer Park Monastery

for Tess Gallagher

The first night, moon full.
Each night after, moon's light

in retreat, darkness standing by,
light held in the curve of space

it holds for itself, until fullness
fades, and the dipper empties

its cargo of stars into
the black cauldron of sky.

We arrive full, bags heavy
with books, heads brimming

with words. Each day
we let go what we can

see beauty in soup bowls,
shaved heads, brown robes.

Days pass in slow step,
moon arcs across the sky.

Then the last night we
walk arm in arm under

a black cloak of stars
share the ginger singe

of Black Black gum,
and stars wink back

each one a poem
we won't need to write.

If the River

After Joan Swift

If the river knew it wasn't telling. If
    the river knew its way, it only muttered
        slick syllables against stone, so we turned

our backs, quit listening. If the river knew the way
    out, mum was the word it never spoke, only breathed,
        cupping each fallen star in its wet arms, mouth full of stones,
            murmuring the ancient stories we no longer heard.

Listen, the river is running, braiding the blues, weaving dark with light,
    stars falling and shattering in its arms, the swift river keeps running,
        keeps holding the fallen, keeps telling the *mustn't tell* stories,
            braiding the tears, the blood, the stirring, the swelling,
                the sweaters that shielded, the sagging sac,
                    the red blossoming, abandoned,

current carrying all that can't be said as words, insistent, nudge mute
    cobbles, all the bodies, the dreams, the shattered stars flowing down
        to where the river weaves the *mustn't tell* with the imagined,
            the unseen, the unheard, the fragile, the tough with the tears,
            the scorned, the overlooked with the bright fallen stars
                into one story *that stays and stays.*

Mosaic

for Terry Tempest Williams

This morning sun shot through cloud shards
as you describe   how   the river whispered
mosaic   how you traveled   to   Italy
to learn   from the artists   were   given
the task   of   breaking   stones   learned
then   light is integral   illuminating
what   we won't see otherwise. You told how
you were invited   to travel   to Rwanda,
how you first said   *No*   your brother
just passed then   heard yourself say   *Yes*.
You went   to Rwanda   met the Hutu
women   their villages destroyed   by Tutsis
while the US debated the definition of genocide
they'd lost everything   they had less   than nothing.
How the women   unwrapped   the bones
of the children   they'd lost   to show you
how they   kept them under   their beds
wrapped in fabric   no land   for a proper burial.
How this artist   created   a memorial
to honor   those bones.   How even
these   broken shards   can be held   up
to the light   how light   finds   its way
through each crack and craze.   How even
this deepest   grief   these shattered   lives
can   through art   be   reassembled.

After Seeing *Photograph 51*

for Rosalind Franklin

25 July 1920 – 16 April 1958

She photographed the dark X of DNA,
        figured how to keep temperature constant,

wanted certainty, not a theory, direct proof
        A & B each twist a double helix, not speculation,

who preferred to work alone—the only woman
        in King's College Lab—what choice did she have

but to bristle at the condescension of Wilkins,
        not get too familiar with Gosling.

I wish I'd been able to see it, she admits, years later,
        recognition long gone to Watson & Crick.

She who loved shapes, who drew patterns as a girl,
        despite her father's plea to *please draw people,*

her gifts spun in her DNA, though she wouldn't
        receive credit until later, years after twin

tumors in her ovaries swelled big as lab sponges.
        Still, she went to the lab each morning to finish

what she'd begun because *that's what scientists do,*
        not knowing her obituary—*dead of ovarian cancer at 37—*

would read *research scientist, spinster, daughter of a banker*
                    as if those words could someday explain

what no woman could have known then, could begin
                    to explain the sacrifices she was making.

Adrift

for Jack Gilbert

Nouns the first to go, even for this poet
for whom words were once all that mattered.
His attendant says he knows the function—
the thing that wakes me, the thing that opens—
but nouns have slipped across
the border, leaving him adrift
in a functional world, metaphors
sunk like soggy life rings, each
remaining name a raft
on the receding horizon,
words jettisoned
daily to keep the body
afloat distilling finally
to this:
the thing I wrote poems with,
and this*:*
the thing that closes.

Each Bird Singing: A Cento

What seas what shores what grey rocks and what islands
and scent of pine and wood thrush singing through the fog.

So you see to reach the past is easy. A snap. A snap of the sea
and a third of a century passes. Good memory,

if you are such a boat, tell me we did not falter
in the vastness when we walked ashore.

I am alone among the others who have stood here
as they looked out over the snowy fields, holding their breath.

What the train and the river were saying, no one could understand.
We just stood there, breathing what was left of the night.

The great light cage has broken up in the air freeing, I think,
about a million birds whose wild ascending shadows will not be back.

Is light the last thing lost or never lost at all?
All's a scattering, a shining.

There is time, still time, for one who can groan to sing,
for one who can sing to be healed.

We must risk delight. Learn the flowers, go light.
Perhaps a speckled dream to wrestle in the night.

Far out in a universe a tomorrow we can't see
is singing the last word of a song we heard long ago.

Sparrow your message is clear: it is not too late for my singing.
With small hope from the center of darkness it calls out again and again.

Four

Tell me. Who was I when I used to call your name?

Marie Howe, *What the Living Do*

*Each of us leaves evidence on the earth
that...bears our form.*

Sally Mann, *Hold Still:
A Memoir with Photographs*

What Daughters Do

Each July peaches arrived in their purple carriages
of tissue, fine jewels inside a wood-slatted crate.
One by one, we'd uncover them, each still warm

from the sun, lay the soft fuzz against our cheek.
Our job: slicing them for pies, what daughters do,
while Mom mixed flour and Crisco for the crust.

I never learned to make pie crust from her. When finally
I ask, it's too late. She stares, puzzled, at the rolling pin,
hands it back to me, *here honey, you do it.*

Today I'm making pie crust, remembering all I saw.
My hands roll out the crust in a full moon, draw it thinner,
more translucent with each stroke, fold it neatly into quarters,

slip it onto the pie plate, unfold the quarters like wings.
Then crimp the crust, thumb nestling between fingers
in arcs until the crust ripples, circling, more continuous

than memory, still claiming its hands.

Subtraction

The countdown begins,
brain loses its hold on the familiar:
spoon, glass now objects to turn
in her hand, hold. Faces blur
and she sees not by sight
but by emotion, sensing who
is with her, how they're feeling,
what do they want her to do
and does she want to do it?
She no longer wears her glasses,
knows how to put on her shoes,
remembers to brush her teeth, to eat,
world telescoping smaller,
belongings that once filled a house
with ten rooms and seven closets
now all contained in a dresser with
three drawers, labeled with her name,
like summer camp, because *everyone*
here takes everyone else's clothes,
the nurses tell us. We fill the room
with flowers, photographs, cards,
try to coax her to stay, bring in
nature videos, *The Sound of Music*,
invite her to sing along. Still, she walks
the halls, restless, stopping to greet us
when we arrive—*are you someone*
I know?—then off on her
mission, whatever it is. So we go
with her on this journey, too,

take her hand, pace these unfamiliar
halls until they become familiar,
until they become just one more
place she will leave behind.

The Bath

The tub fills inch by inch,
as I kneel beside it, trail my fingers

in the bright braid of water.
Mom perches on the toilet seat,

entranced by the ritual until
she realizes the bath's for her.

Oh no, she says, drawing her
three layers of shirts to her chest,

crossing her arms and legs.
Oh no, I couldn't, she repeats,

brow furrowing, that look I now
recognize like an approaching squall.

I abandon reason, the hygiene argument,
promise a Hershey's bar, if she will just,

please, take off her clothes. *Oh no,*
she repeats, her voice rising.

Meanwhile, the water is cooling.
I strip off my clothes, step into it,

let the warm water take me
completely, slipping down until

only my face shines up, a moon mask.
Mom stays with me, interested now

in this turn of events. I sit up.
Will you wash my back, Mom?

So much gone, but let this
still be there. She bends over

to dip the washcloth in the still
warm water, squeezes it,

lets it dribble down my back,
leans over to rub the butter pat

of soap, swiping each armpit,
then rinses off the suds with long

practiced strokes. I turn around
to thank her, catch her smiling,

lips pursed, humming,
still a mother with a daughter

whose back needs washing.

Whatever Remains

It's just that I can't help her, he says

my father, a doctor for forty years
in our small town, who made

house calls after other doctors
stopped, his ankles creaking

as he slipped past my bedroom
and down the stairs. My father

can't save my mother, his wife
of fifty years, from this journey

into fog, though he goes to see
her each day, feeds her lunch

next to the man who sings
You are my sunshine to his wife,

who lies in a recliner,
hasn't spoken for a year.

They hover there at the table,
spoons poised and gleaming

ready to scoop up what's
left, whatever remains.

Eight Years Later

You brought the sun back after weeks away
and I take that as a sign you're still out there
looking after us, still trying to order the weather
into compliance, never content to let the day

unfold without some prompting—
oh, I wish it wouldn't cloud over—and I hear
your words in mine, willing the sun to break
through the gloom, as if that might restore

a shimmer, might yet make us all happy.
Eight years ago, when we carried you to your grave
high on the bluffs above the Mississippi,
the sun broke through billowing clouds,

radiant and fierce like your moods that
terrified me as a kid—and what else
could you do, wife of a doctor in
a conservative Midwestern town,

but try to rule the weather? Dad joined you
last month, six inches of snow falling
the day of his service, but when we filed
out of the church singing *Take me out to the ballgame,*

the snow was backlit by a flash, then off
in the distance, a grumble of thunder,
and we knew you were there, greeting
your husband, still wanting the last word.

Geometry

The sun's circle drops to the flat line
of horizon, suddenly cords and arcs,

fire swallowed by water. We walk back
up the beach, shells crunching under our feet.

You lean on my arm, hold in your other hand
a walking stick—a gift from my sister—carved

from exotic hardwoods. We round
the curve of beach just as the moon pops

above the skyline, a released balloon,
climbs untethered into the sky. I turn

as the skimmers descend to feed,
black wings arched, open their beaks,

cut widening Vs in the darkening sea,
see then our path: two sets of footprints

welling with water and between,
a long trail of ellipses.

Measurements

Was it the turkey, cooked fifteen minutes too long,
despite the thermometer thrust into its gullet?
Or should we blame the mashed potatoes,

russets stripped of the thin millimeter of earthy skin?
Perhaps the stuffing—boxed—laced
with five grams of sodium? Maybe the gravy,

lumping, without its ¼ cup of *roux*?
And so we gather here to give thanks
for what—we're no longer sure—

the food before us, yes, but when did
this dinner veer off course? When did we stop
being grateful, want instead to be right?

How to measure the moment love flees
instead of stays? What are the rest of us to do
now but raise our glasses, lift our forks,

eat and drink as if nothing happened,
as if no one just slammed a door, drove off,
empty plate luminous as the gibbous moon.

As if we don't know all the ways we try
to gauge love, all the ways
we don't always measure up.

Scarlet Hibiscus Blooming

Five years since we walked this beach
with my mother, laughed as she imitated
the royal terns, their bad hair days.

I was grateful for your kindness as her mind
departed, for the games of shuffleboard,
walks in the garden, she a giddy girl again,

scarlet hibiscus blooming in her grey hair.
Love, it's not that we won't grow old;
we will, our bodies worn like shells

in the surf. It's not that you can save me,
as I once hoped you could. It's not that I fear
dying, though of course I do. It's the slow diminish-

ment, ebb of wonder, of heart-catching joy
and terror as we show each other our hands,
whatever we're willing, as we become more

known, more loved, more achingly alone.

Secretariat Redux

"He was the color of burnished wire and could race a hole through the wind."

We're rewatching the Disney version, can forgive the melodrama
because of that final scene, when Secretariat rounds the track

at Belmont, pulls ahead of Sham, not just one length or two,
when Secretariat just keeps running, hooves pummeling red dirt,

all the other horses falling back, no longer in the race, when it's clear
he's running for no reason but joy, not the jockey, a burr on his back.

As he rounds the last turn, defying the odds, I'm eighteen again,
just out of high school, down in the basement with my dad

watching on our 12-inch set. I'm remembering how seeing
Secretariat lean into the stretch made my father, the quiet doctor,

whoop and holler, a horse that carried not just the hopes
of a tattered country, but the inchoate dreams of a generation

who worked hard, not knowing another way to provide
but to just keep rounding the track. See now

how much still rides on that copper colt's back.

Walking with Our Fathers

for John G. Pierce and Sidney O. Hughes

In his last days your father walked the boardwalk
that ran above the sea, sat on the bench looking west,

watched for the snow goose that overwintered one year,
could still name his beloved birds—*curlew, plover, dunlin*—

when other words had flown. He flew, too,
two springs ago. My father slipped out

two weeks ago, a light snow falling
out the window of the room in the hospital

where he'd cared for others all his life.
Tell me, love, are we ever ready to let our fathers fly?

Were we ready to fledge or did we just fall
from the nest, not look back 'til now,

wonder what more we might have said,
wonder who'll tell the tired jokes now,

who'll join us to walk this beach—
here at the western edge of the continent,

where the sea brings news from Japan,
and the sky holds its breath—

where we could walk for days
listening to the surf roll in,

watching it erase every step.

Kingfisher's Vigil

for Betty Pierce

Your son wings down a stormy coast
as I lap the beach, wondering
how you'll be when he arrives.

Will you survive this week of pain—
small bones of your spine disintegrating,
nerves fraying, messages not getting through

to body, family, friends. *What will it mean?*
Will you be able to go home? We all knew
this was ahead; we have no choice but to walk

this path—as I did when my mother's mind flew
before her body. But so much rests on this love:
your love for your son, which enables love for me,

love you share with your brood, all sheltered under
your generous wings. And they're all walking with me
as we thank you for the gift, for generations that will

flourish because you raised your children well.
At the end of the beach two jet contrails cross,
and closer, kingfisher zigzags out to the snag

where he watches for a glint of what can't be seen,
except from above. When your spirit needs to fly,
he'll be there, keeping vigil, reminding us

to keep looking out for those we love.

Meusings

When an animal, a rabbit, say, beds down in a protecting fencerow, the weight and warmth of his curled body leaves a mirroring mark upon the groun....this body-formed evidence of hare, has a name, an obsolete but beautiful word: meuse.

Sally Mann, *Hold Still: A Memoir with Photographs*

Seven months since your mother died,
artifacts from her travels linger on shelves, books
gather dust, drawers with their bent spoons,
shoes with their sprung tongues, the way objects arc

toward dissolution, entropy a law nothing escapes
though we try, dusting the books, polishing the silver,
watering the ficus. One by one, we sidle up to the
mission paintings, soapstone carvings, Navaho pottery.

No one wants to be the first to stake a claim.
So we slip from turned bowl to bird figurine,
recounting each story, knowing its time has come,
that even your mother—who always traveled light—

couldn't carry on her beloved birds.
See how they flock, uncertain, on the shelf,
awaiting the cues to migrate,
not sure when or where to fly.

Taking Down the Paintings

for Sarah, John, Anne, and James

One by one, we take down the paintings,
each with its back story, signed by the artist,
its quiet middle finger to mortality,
insistence that art endure,
beauty matters, that we can dodge death
for one more decade,

maybe two, with luck. But the decades
wing past, kingfishers trapped in flight, painted
on pottery, trivets, etched in stone, and death
not yet on *our* minds. We wonder about the artists:
are they prosperous or starving? Will their legacy endure
as long as this painting? We'd wondered when mortality

would don a capital M, not a stylish beret. Now Mortality
strides into our lives, the word we'd avoided all these decades,
letting our parents take their turn, endure
the slings and arrows; *we* won't get painted
into a corner. So we turn to art: let the artists
do what artists do best: express the unexpressed, defy death

in every hue: one painting's ghostly cross glorifies death,
while orange poppies on a hillside shout *endure*—
and they will. Even unknown artists seize the day, paint
their way to slippery immortality,
one more disappearing decade
before throwing down the trowel, artists

all to the end. But aren't we *all* artists
re-creating ourselves to endure?
Please, just a few decades
more, we bargain. *Block death*
at the door! Today, we offer Mortality
a seat at the table, remove each painting

with a sigh, release the artist to her easel, nod to Death,
promise to endure together whatever Mortality
has in store. And lean the paintings, decades deep, by the door.

Here, Now, Listen: Letter to Rags from Tieton

I'm sitting on the deck of the Harvest Hall in late
September sun. This January, six years since you left,

and still I see this world through your eyes. Looking out
through warped single-paned windows of the hall

as the aspens shimmy in the wind, I remember
you'd replace broken panes with colored glass

so gazing up through the tall window behind
the woodstove pipe was a kaleidoscope of color

as the cedars slowly swayed outside. *Here, now,* you'd say,
listen, as the church bell chimes noon, a dog barks,

trash can lid rattles. In the alley, a car rumbles to life
and a magpie struts past, spreading his piano key wings.

If you were here, we'd walk to the bakery,
drink weak coffee from old china cups, wipe

our fingers on dime store napkins, then stroll
around the square, find a wood bench in the sun.

You'd nod off under your tweed hat, wake with a start,
smile to find me here, reach for my hand, then draw

slowly to your feet. Together, we'd track the magpie,
so intent in this act you lose the world; that's when

I know you're still here—*there,* when the magpie shows
his hand and the old song of the world starts up again.

What You'd Give

for Rags on his 97th birthday

We've celebrated your birthday together
for 20 years now and most years I'm late,
driving fast to arrive at last to find you
reading by the fire, lost in one of many
lives you lived—stringer for *Time*,
foreign correspondent in World War II,
White House Press Corps,
beloved journalism professor.

Today I arrive to lamb in the oven,
red potatoes boiling, green beans
from the farmer's market steaming
and you at the table by the window
in your striped French sailor shirt,
faded jeans held up by red suspenders,
light in your eyes bright but flickering,
clouds scudding past summer sun.

After dinner, we walk up the road
under Douglas firs you refuse
to cut, though they tower high
over your cabin, could crush it
in the next storm. Farther up,
the glade of chestnuts you planted
on my first visit now offer shade.

I remember that day, turning to wave
as you tucked a chestnut into the
furrowed earth. We walk past
each fruit tree you planted that spring—
pear, apple, green gage plum—
lugging water in five-gallon buckets
up the driveway until they
could survive on their own.

So little I knew then of the care needed
for trees to thrive, of what it took to tend
even my own life. Your life the one
I wanted, caught on the restless
treadmill of youth, never dreaming
what you'd give me someday would be this:
it's the care & feeding, the watering & tending—
these daily rituals that make up a life.

Five

If there is a world, let me be in it.
Let fires arise and pass…
Let the old hopes be made new.
Let stacks of clouds blacken if they have to
but never let the people in this town go hungry.…
If there is a world where we feel very little,
let it not be our world.

Joanna Klink,
Excerpts from a Secret Prophecy

Credo

Make a place for the glint in the seal's eye that second before
it rolls back its slick head, slips silent beneath the surface.

Make room for the shimmer of salmon, splitting the sun, leaping
for the stream of its birth, even knowing what's ahead.

Carve out a corner for the crab who grasped the blade
of the cleaver that sliced it in two, wouldn't let go.

That light, dazzling dark sea ahead, remember it, remember
how it seeps from billowing cumulus when you least expect

or how the sun finds the crack in the horizon's solder to empty
out its cargo at dusk, a slick sheen across the water.

How the green spinning earth and blue brimming sea go on and on
even when we're not looking, and that perhaps, if we can pay

attention for even a second, remember just this—it may not
make us whole, but it could be a good place to begin.

Pantoum for Tahlequah

I can't sleep and when I dream, I dream of her
carrying her daughter for 17 days,
swimming the dark waters of the Salish Sea,
dark sea that carries us all equally.

She will carry her daughter 17 days,
bearing her grief, searching for salmon
the dark sea that carries us all equally,
in these waters, her birthright.

She bears her grief as they search for salmon,
swims past the bays where their mothers were taken,
in these waters, their birthright,
these waters that glisten, hide sewage and toxins.

Swims past the bays where their mothers were taken,
up the coast they've long swum,
these waters that glisten, hide sewage and toxins,
carrying grief she can't set down.

Up the coast, fewer each year, they swim.
Does she feel grief for her pod as they face what's ahead?
Carrying grief she won't set down,
in this sea where they hunted, quiet, alone.

Is it grief for her species facing extinction
in a warming sea that first was their home,
this sea where they hunted quiet, alone.
She carries our grief, what we can't set down

in this warming sea that was first their home;
how long will she carry her grief—
our grief, what we can't set down—
that we are changing our world and theirs.

How long will we bear this grief,
her grief and ours, that
we've changed our world and theirs?
How long can we carry this on?

Against Apocalypse

No more crying over spilt milk, turned wine, over rain
that won't fall, over calendar pages leafing the wind

as decades blow past, wind that once lifted tenderly
each blade of grass now taking down towns.

Meanwhile, the earth spins on her axis, day and night arrive
on schedule, but seasons on strike, certainties flown

with the birds, ocean lapping, hungry at the shore.
Why do so few say it: *the end of the world at hand.*

Still we post photos of risotto, take selfies
at the beach of our bodies buried in the sand.

We hunker down with YouTube, binge
on Netflix, take up Zumba. Meanwhile

politicians lead us like lemmings for the cliffs,
while the rest freeze in future's brights.

Meanwhile, the earth keeps spinning. Sun rises & sets.
Civilizations come & go. We won't be the first,

though we may be the last. But remember your neighbor,
who showed up with a pot of chicken soup, still steaming,

the day you lost power. Another who shoveled you out,
drove you to the ferry in his battered four-wheel drive.

Who knows what's ahead: fast burn or slow freeze;
asteroids, black holes, exploding galaxies?

If someday none of us can see the sun,
remember this: the world you want to inhabit.

Rising

But out of such persistence arose turtles, rivers,
mitochondria, figs—all this resinous, unretractable earth.

Jane Hirshfield, "Optimism"

Each day seas rise, pterapods release
spiraling wings, swirl together

in the dervish of dissolving beings
as jellyfish gather, mass and drift.

What about that idealism we carried
all those years unsinged? It's not too

late to hold fast to what sustains,
even as it sinks from sight:

steadiness of stones,
grasses riffling wind,

bright eye of flicker at the window,
bat's outstretched, translucent wing,

each shuddering strand of spiderweb,
each resilient vine and tendril.

Send down resinous roots,
connect deep underground,

enduring, invisible, quietly
rising, resisting threads of mycelium.

Elemental

Early sun lights each square prayer flag
as it shudders in the wind: red, green, yellow—
primary colors—we learned in elementary school.
What is primary, what is elemental but this?
The grey cat stretched on a terracotta deck,
eyes closed, tail twitching, dreams of mice.
The red dog back from his morning walk,
kibble in his belly, asleep on a green blanket,
whimpers, dreams of rabbits. Me wearing
blue fleece, watching a spiderweb take shape,
perfect in its trembling symmetry, each strand
shimmering. And the golden spider at the heart
of its work, resting, lit by sun, as we all hang
together, shuddering light and shadow.

Heading Home

for Tom Jay

We meet at the Farm's Reach Café, drive south on Center,
park by the stream rippling through burnished alders.

Tom climbs into Farmer Johns, then into the pen
teeming with a late run of summer chums,

wearing cotton gloves so he won't leave a scent.
Carefully, he dips the net, scoops up four in the first load,

calls out *female, female, male, male*, then lifts the net
over the pen, lets the salmon ease back

into the stream they know by smell, scoops out
another salmon, then another until just a handful remain.

I climb in, stand in cold water up to my thighs, lower the net
into the darkest corner. *That'll be a female*, Tom predicts.

They're all females now. I carefully lift each one,
release her into fast water, watch her race up the riffles,

feel my blood stir in that ancient dance I swear I knew,
once, so long ago, almost forgotten but not yet gone:

fins fluttering, we're all heading home at last.

Chimacum Valley Suite

i.   Walking, Dawn
This morning, fog hangs
in the valley as cows low
to each other, adrift
in the fields like whales
echolocating, ships navigating
the fog banks. *I'm here,* one calls.
we are too, we answer.

ii.   Compost
Earth, straw, seeds, rain.
From so little squash
takes off, running,
honking her golden horn.

iii.   Talisman
Heirloom tomatoes still dream
of summer as I pick them, green
for jam. One drops to the ground
and I carry it for days in my pocket,
pull it out to sniff when I need
a shot of summer not yet gone.

iv.   Walking, Dusk
Crows fly over, inspecting
the fields, return to light
in the muscled arms of the tree
perched at the edge of the ditch
where still a few apples hang
like cast off, rusty ornaments.

One stabs what's left of an apple,
flies off across the valley with four
in pursuit, weaving and diving
like stunt pilots as we watch,
cheering them on. Just when
we're all drunk on late season

apples, on fall's fleeting
light, the sun drops below
the ridge, and the crows
careen down the road,
slick black wings refracting
the last rays of light.

One Last Whiff

Mid-October, and I'm not ready to give up
on my heirloom tomatoes, too late to ripen
this summer that broke all records for cool days.

I kneel, take one last whiff of short-
lived summer, twist each from its stem,
round green bodies hard in my palms,

wash & pat them dry. With the sharpest knife,
chop them into shards, sweep them into the blue bowl,
sprinkle with lemon juice, brown sugar, cinnamon.

In the morning, stir again, then boil, simmer, cool.
We spoon the chunky jam into jars, set them
on the shelf in the pantry, listen for the *ping, ping, ping*

of lids sealing, saying *now, it is time, you must let it go.*

Farm Tour the Day Before Equinox

Finnriver Farm

We are here to glean what's left
of summer, sun sliding on across the fields,
up the long valley, its endless farewell.

Here, blueberry bushes hold summer
in green branches, nets flung over
to save them from crows who plot

in the firs. We walk down the hill,
plastic pail in hand, to pick
what's left, whatever remains.

At first, the berries hard to see,
but reaching into the heart
of the bush, we find each

quiet one on its thin stem. Then,
blueberry picking meditation:
not too fast or you'll knock them off,

just one small berry after the next,
hand moving from sky to earth,
bush to bucket, an arc that completes

summer, that will carry us
into fall. For now, we are alone
with each last second of summer,

picking each berry as if our lives depend
on it, holding it carefully, tenderly,
before dropping it into the bucket.

Swimming into Fall

Each day chills like butter in a well,
    sky deepens without summer's veil.
       I enter the water slowly,
          steeped in gold like tea,
            arms and legs sliding
              into the familiar motion,
                 stroking out to the far shore
                 where tall reeds wait
                  below chattering aspen,
                  to the lanky stems of lily pads
                  slick with algae, and in this way,
                  I swim back into summer,
                  holding on with each stroke,
                  each exhaling drift of bubbles
                  until the water is swimming me
                  in its golden fins. At last,
                 I can breathe without sadness—
              fall—one season tilting into the next
            and this could be enough:
          to move without thought
        where sun mottles shadow.
       I towel dry, the sun moves on,
      children's voices peal far off, and the
     line of a fisherman snakes gold,
   catching the last of summer
  with each cast before settling
onto the darkening surface.

After 22 Years, Astilbe

for John

In those getting-to-know-you days,
we lined up your writers: Carver, Harrison,
Nabokov against mine: Gallagher, Levertov,
Le Guin. But we agreed on Merwin as we agreed
on forget-me-nots, bachelor buttons.

I wanted what was barely tame back then,
letting even buttercups have their way.
You were the careful pruner, trusting
that everything responds to gentle touch
in time, while I scattered wildflower seeds

with abandon to see what might come up,
refused to trim the jasmine, honeysuckle,
wisteria until they were climbing the roof.
Our first argument, if you can call it that,
was over the astilbe you wanted to plant.

Not in my garden, I protested, drawing the line,
envisioning domesticity's insidious creep.
Twenty-two years later, I give you an astilbe,
at last grown into our shared garden, finally
wise enough to trust your gentle hand.

Leavings

Today, rain falls on us all equally:
crab grass, hawk huddled in a hemlock,
field mouse he watches with a quick

gold eye. Like so many days before,
I take out the compost, empty
the day's leavings: egg shells, coffee

grounds, all fodder for the days
ahead. Like so many days before, I go
to the window, see the camellia's leaves

glisten, watch the cat who watches the finches
as they vie for dark, oily seeds. Come
evening, we spread summer's harvest

of lavender on newspapers, run stiff stems
between our fingers as we listen to Dylan Thomas
read *A Child's Christmas in Wales*, his rich

syllables flowing like syrup until our fingers ache
and lavender hangs in the air thick
with all we've not yet spoken.

A week out of surgery, still riding the relief
the tumor was benign, even with a brain
blurred by oxycodone. Only the cats' steady

breathing, and when our hands stray
against each other, careless again,
I can at last rest in the blessed everyday.

Past Dusk

taking the last lap toward home,
steady chant of the right turn signal,
darkness rising from the firs, this stretch
I know in my bones, its bend and sway.
Meanwhile, mind wanders back up the trail,
what was said, what wasn't, *how much more
do we have to give? This or that good cause
but it's all the same—the world careening—*
then round the bend, gold eyes trapped
in headlight's stare from the ditch,
one wing slowly lifts.

Whose breath do I breathe in?

Wait for the other wing to lift,
heart jackhammering in the cage
of my chest, beg her please to fly,
wonder what I'll do if she can't—*oh
what I would give, what I would give up—*
when she unfolds both wings, rises
out of the dark ditch, swoops low over us,
cream feathers of her breast close enough
to caress, wings lifting, falling like breath
in the quiet spring night and we inhale,
exhale, fly up the road together
into the blessed uncertain night.

Oak Bay the Last Day of the Year

Tide's running hard when we reach the beach.
Fox wobbles, sniffs the air, and we settle

onto a drift log to bask in brief winter sun.
So many walks here this year on this spit,

tangle of briny marsh grass. We both
wonder, don't ask, *how many more*?

On the horizon, Tahoma hovers,
impassive as the year we'll soon enter, ready

or not. A heron lifts his ponderous wings,
raises and lowers them three times, flying

up the channel so slowly he'll surely fall
from the sky. Scoters and harlequins scatter

& wheel above a bright running sea, settle
back as if one, wings bright & backlit.

You hold a cold hand to my cheek:
Love, no knowing what the next will bring.

NOTES

"68th Anniversary of the Bikini": Based on a National Public Radio story that aired July 17, 2014.

"Remember the Flood of '65": Dedicated to Nancy Taylor's father, who with other engineers saved my hometown of Winona, Minnesota that year.

"For the Last Roll of Kodachrome": Based on an National Public Radio story that aired December 29, 2010.

"Send in the Clown": Based on a news story published in the *New York Times* in January 2017.

"March 6, 1890: Eugene Shieffelin Releases 80 Starlings in Central Park": Based on an article by Kim Todd in *Orion,* Winter 1998.

"Shishi Odoshi": Dedicated to Sue Sutherland-Hanson, dear colleague, fine poet, and beloved friend, who left us too early, and who told me the Japanese word for "deer scare," which became the title of this poem.

"Doors": Written for Robert Hedin at the Anderson Center in Red Wing, Minnesota, the year after he'd retired as director.

"Walking Gary Snyder's Dog": Written at Fishtrap during the Summer Gathering 2010, when Gary Snyder was keynote speaker.

"Moon Phases at Deer Park Monastery": Written during a week at Deer Park Monastery with Tess Gallagher in 1996.

"If the River": The lines in italics are taken from "Stillaquamish Flood" in Joan Swift's last book, *The Body That Follows Us,* published posthumously by Cave Moon Press in 2017.

"After Seeing *Photograph 51":* Written after seeing a moving production of this play at the Seattle Repertory Theatre in 2013.

"Adrift": Written after meeting Jack Gilbert in a memory care facility in Berkeley, CA, while on reading tour for *Beyond Forgetting: Poems & Prose about Alzheimer's Disease.*

"Each Bird Singing: A Cento": Thanks to Linda Bierds for her inspiration to try this form. The lines are taken from: Elizabeth Bishop, T.S. Eliot, Tess Gallagher, Jack Gilbert, Robert Hedin, Tom Jay, Galway Kinnell, Ted Kooser, Theodore Roethke, Joan Swift, and Gary Snyder.

"Here, Now, Listen: Letter to Rags from Tieton": Written in Melissa Swasny's class at LitFuse in June 2014 for a widely beloved journalism professor and my close friend and mentor, Wilmott Ragsdale, who his friends knew as "Rags."

"Heading Home": This poem is dedicated to Tom Jay—sculptor, essayist, poet, word lover, community activist, salmon stream restorer—who headed home as this book goes to press, joining the fall chum run he was instrumental in restoring during a record year.

ACKNOWLEDGMENTS

Alaska Quarterly Review Fall/Winter 2004: "The Bath"

America Zen: A Gathering of Poets (anthology): "Mind Wanting More"

Becoming: What Makes a Woman (anthology): "The Bath"

Beyond Forgetting: Poetry & Prose about Alzheimer's Disease (anthology): "The Bath"

Cirque, vol. 9 #1, Winter 2018: "If the River" (Tribute to Joan Swift)

Clover, vol. 5, Summer 2013: "Memory, take me back," "Walking with Our Fathers"

Clover, vol. 6, Fall 2013: "Measurements"

Crosscurrents, 2012: "Re-reading Tu Fu Thirty Years Later," "For the Last Roll of Kodachrome"

Crosscurrents, 2013: "E O Y Z P"

Dancing with Joy: 99 Poems (anthology): "Mind Wanting More"

Family Matters: Poems of our Families (anthology): "What Daughters Do"

Fire on Her Tongue (anthology): "Approaching 52"

For Love of Orcas: An Anthology: "Pantoum for Tahlequah"

Poetry of Presence: An Anthology of Mindfulness Poems (anthology): "Mind Wanting More"

Pontoon 3: "March 6, 1890: Eugene Shieffelin Releases 80 Starlings in Central Park"

Pontoon 6: "The Bath"

SpiritFirst, 2012: "Credo"

The Poets Guide to the Birds: "March 6, 1890: Eugene Shieffelin Releases 80 Starlings in Central Park"

Via Regia: "Elemental" (titled "Prayer for Facing Fall")

Windfall, Fall 2011: "Farm Tour the Day Before Equinox"

Windfall, Spring 2012: "Cape Disappointment"

"Cape Disappointment" is included on the Washington Poetic Routes website curated by Washington State Poet Laureate Claudia Castro-Luna. https://washingtonpoeticroutes.com/

"*Shishi Odoshi*" and "Elemental" (titled "Primary Colors") were printed as broadsides by The North Press in Port Townsend, Washington. http://thenorthpress.website/

GRATITUDE

These poems were written over many decades and with the support of my village—family, friends, and colleagues too many to name here— my deep gratitude to each of you.

Thanks to John Willson and Bethany Reid for feedback on early drafts and for sustaining me through busy years of teaching with our correspondence. The Village Idioms and Kingston Poets provided inspiration that endured long after we stopped meeting.

Tess Gallagher, Kathleen Flenniken, Katie Humes, and Carmen Germaine each provided valuable feedback at different stages of the manuscript.

As always, a deep bow of gratitude to Stan Sanvel Rubin and the late Judith Kitchen, cofounders of Pacific Lutheran University's low-residency MFA program, the Rainier Writing Workshop; in addition, to current director Rick Barot, and the faculty, students, and alumni of RWW for providing a lively writing community that continues to sustain me.

And to Tess, as always, for first encouraging me down the path of poetry and for many decades of inspiration since we met on the deck of *Crusader,* both for her work and her life.

I'm grateful to residencies over the years that have offered invaluable time and space as well as solitude and community: Centrum, Hedgebrook, the Whiteley Center, Artsmith, Vermont Studio Center, Anderson Center, H.J. Andrews Forest, and Playa.

Gratitude to Michael Daley for his seasoned editorial eye, patience, and many good conversations about poetry along the way. Thanks to book designer Nina Noble for her elegant design, to artist Zann Jacobrown for her painting on the cover, and to fellow Empty Bowl poets for their friendship and inspiration.

Finally, deepest gratitude to John Pierce for caring about commas and for sticking with me.

ABOUT HOLLY J. HUGHES

Photo by Cynthia Neubecker

Holly J. Hughes is the author of *Passings*, which received an American Book Award from the Before Columbus Foundation in 2017. She is also the author of *Sailing by Ravens*, co-author of *The Pen and The Bell: Mindful Writing in a Busy World*, and editor of the award-winning anthology, *Beyond Forgetting: Poetry and Prose about Alzheimer's Disease.* Her poems and essays have been nominated for a Pushcart prize and have appeared in many anthologies, including *Poetry of Presence: An Anthology of Mindfulness Poems, Dancing with Joy: 99 Poems, Working the Woods, Working the Sea,* and *The Poets Guide to Birds.*

Hughes served on the staff of Pacific Lutheran University's low-residency MFA program for 12 years and taught writing for more than 25 years at Edmonds Community College, as well as at regional conferences and workshops, among them Fishtrap, Kachemak Bay Writer's Conference, Litfuse, the North Cascades Institute, and Write on the Sound. She also spent over thirty summers working on the water in Alaska, commercial fishing for salmon, skippering a 65-foot schooner, and working as a naturalist on ships. She currently teaches writing and mindfulness workshops in Alaska and the Pacific Northwest and consults as a writing coach, dividing her time between a home in the Chimacum valley and a log cabin built in the 1930s in Indianola, Washington. hollyjhughes.com